**COACH YOURSELF
BETTER, FAST**

WRITE TO THINK

Based on *Exploratory Writing: Everyday magic for life and work* by Alison Jones

First published in Great Britain by Practical Inspiration Publishing, 2024

© Alison Jones and Practical Inspiration Publishing, 2024

The moral rights of the author have been asserted

ISBN   978-1-78860-664-6 (paperback)
978-1-78860-666-0 (epub)
978-1-78860-665-3 (Kindle)

All rights reserved. This book, or any portion thereof, may not be reproduced without the express written permission of the publisher.

Every effort has been made to trace copyright holders and to obtain their permission for the use of copyright material. The publisher apologizes for any errors or omissions and would be grateful if notified of any corrections that should be incorporated in future reprints or editions of this book.

Want to bulk-buy copies of this book for your team and colleagues? We can customize the content and co-brand *Write to Think* to suit your business's needs.

Please email info@practicalinspiration.com for more details.

Practical Inspiration Publishing

Contents

Series introduction iv
Introduction 1
Day 1: Attention 12
Day 2: Instinctive elaboration 19
Day 3: Inquiry 25
Day 4: Storytelling 34
Day 5: Sensemaking 40
Day 6: Reframing 48
Day 7: Empathy 55
Day 8: Metaphor 59
Day 9: Visual thinking 67
Day 10: Reflective practice 80
Conclusion 87
List of prompts 89
Endnotes 94

Series introduction

Welcome to *6-Minute Smarts*!

This is a series of very short books with one simple purpose: to introduce you to ideas that can make life and work better, and to give you time and space to think about how those ideas might apply to *your* life and work.

Each book introduces you to ten powerful ideas, but ideas on their own are useless – that's why each idea is followed by self-coaching questions to help you work out the 'so what?' for you in just six minutes of exploratory writing. Because that's where the magic happens.

Whatever you're facing, there's a *6-Minute Smarts* book just for you. And once you've learned how to coach yourself through a new idea, you'll be smarter for life.

Find out more...

Introduction

Do you love a workshop? I love a workshop. It's all high-energy creative thinking, problem-solving, emotional intelligence exercises, visioning and so on – and it's usually led by an expert who facilitates and guides it all.

Which is great... right up to the point where they leave the room and you're left to carry on the work yourself.

The good news is that once you have the right mindset and a few techniques under your belt, exploratory writing, the kind of writing you'll be discovering in this book, is a way of accessing that big-thinking, workshopping, creative zone whenever you feel like it. And even, sometimes, when you don't.

In a sense, an exploratory writing habit is a complement to any self-development tool you've ever learned, or any you'll ever learn from now on.

An exploratory writing session gives you immediate access to your own personal workshop – or even retreat – wherever and whenever you need it.

And if you often find yourself turning to artificial intelligence (AI) for answers that you *know* really need human intelligence – specifically *your* human intelligence – then this is a great way to engage your brain before you start crafting prompts for a machine.

What's so different about exploratory writing?

If you're in business, you probably do quite a bit of writing. You write emails, sales copy, reports, executive summaries, blog posts, operations documents, memos and more. And each time you write, you're seeking to inform and/or influence your reader. You are, in effect, performing.

What I'm hoping to do here is to get you to see writing in a completely different way. Rather than a public performance space, I want you to see the blank page as uncharted terrain, as an opportunity for you to explore what you *don't* know, rather than simply expressing what you *do*.

I've spoken to hundreds of successful authors in *The Extraordinary Business Book Club* podcast, and they've given lots of super-practical tips on how to write great

Introduction

books. But I very soon started to notice something I hadn't expected: almost without exception, each of them said, in effect, that they wrote not primarily to communicate, but to help them think.

Dave Coplin, former Chief Envisaging Officer at Microsoft, put it like this: 'When you're trying to create something, when you're trying to change something, when you're trying to think differently about something, writing for me is the way that you unravel the spaghetti... and you end up with some really clear, precise thinking that is actionable, that moves the thing forward.'[1]

Dan Pink, author of multiple *New York Times* bestsellers, said much the same: 'Writing is a form of figuring it out. And in fact for me, sometimes it's essential. It's like, "What do you think about this?" "I don't know, I haven't written about it yet."'[2]

And author and book coach Cathy Rentzenbrink put it this way: 'Writing provides a space in which you can spend quite a lot of time working out for yourself what it is you think and feel about things before there's any temptation or obligation to share those opinions with other people.'[3]

Some authors took this even further: they didn't just write to clarify their thinking, they told me, but to go further upstream, into the murky area of pre-verbal thought – impressions, sensations, ideas.

Coach and author Michael Neill probably put it most poetically: '[Writing] forces me to give form to the formless... it makes me put words to the music. Then you've got a song... I can live it and then when I put words to it I can see it, and then as quickly as possible I want to forget the words and go back to living it. It's richer on the other side for having written it.'[4]

So it's clear that many people who write books see the process of writing as being just as much about thinking as it is about communicating, if not more so.

And guess what? You don't have to be writing a book to make this work for you.

If you're a leader or an entrepreneur, or frankly anyone dealing with modern work life, exploratory writing is one of the most flexible and lightweight tools at your disposal for sensemaking, creativity, collaboration, managing stress and overwhelm, and communicating more effectively.

In this book I'm consciously focusing on everyday life and work: if you want to learn how to use writing to address trauma or mental illness, there are lots of great books written by more qualified specialists that will help.

Introduction

But if you're grappling with everyday frustrations – you're in the right place. I hope that you too will discover the freedom and possibilities of the blank page, the excitement of starting a sentence when you have no idea how it's going to end, and the subversive creative joy of being able to write anything because nobody's watching.

If you were to stop reading now, having understood that simply writing when you don't know what it is you want to say is a great way of discovering new things, and start using that in your everyday life, that would be a result.

But I've got an even better idea: I want you to discover it for yourself.

Sounds good. What do I need?

You don't need much, but there are a few things you can't do without when it comes to exploratory writing. They're not exactly specialist equipment...

Essential kit

- A pen or pencil.
- A big scruffy pad of paper (more on this below).

- Somewhere comfortable to write.
- Some way of timing yourself.
- No distractions – from people or devices – during that time.

What else might you like?

- A nice notebook for capturing insights/actions in a more presentable way.
- Tea. And maybe a biscuit.

When do you do it?

Whenever you damn well like. First thing in the morning is good, mostly because it helps you set the direction for your day before everyone else starts trying to get a piece of you. Evening is also good as a way of reflecting on and processing the experiences of the day. But any time you feel the need for a bit of space and clarity is a good time for exploratory writing.

How long do you do it for?

Great question. On the one hand, the answer is of course similar to that for when you should do it,

Introduction

namely as long as you damn well like. Not every exploratory writing session needs to have a deadline. But I've found a deadline is helpful, not least because it focuses my attention and helps me write more quickly, and speed is one of the best ways of breaking through the invisible barrier between what we know we know and what we don't know we know.

For me, six minutes is about as long as I can keep up a true freewriting sprint, by which I mean writing at the speed of thought without stopping, before my energy – or my hand – drops off.

I started my daily exploratory writing practice with a target of ten minutes and discovered that I failed more often than I succeeded. Ten minutes just seemed more than I could spare on a busy day. So I reduced my goal to five minutes – 'I don't care how busy you are, Alison, you can find five minutes.' And I could, most days. Not only that, but the short timescale helped me to focus, to write more quickly and therefore more freely.

But the problem is that it takes most people two or three minutes to get going with exploratory writing, which means that if your session is only five minutes long, you only really have two or three minutes for the good stuff. (In this, I find writing is a little like running: the first few minutes are always dreadful.)

And then I read Gillie Bolton's *Reflective Practice*, in which she recommends six minutes as the optimum sprint time, and when I tried it I was converted.[5] Six minutes feels just as doable as five, but you get a whole extra minute of good stuff. It's a high-yield additional investment of 60 seconds.

So while it's entirely up to you, I'd strongly recommend you start by setting a timer for six minutes. If when it goes off you want to carry on, that's great. But you don't have to.

How often do you do it?

Again, it's tempting to say as often as you like. But let me put the argument for consistency. I run every day. I don't run very far most days, and I don't run very fast, ever. But as I write this in September 2024 I've run every day for over 2,300 days, and I don't plan to stop until circumstances force me to (as one day they inevitably will). Until then I have a non-negotiable daily habit that makes me happier and healthier (and that the dog loves even more than I do).

Doing something every day is known as 'streaking'. (This has nothing to do with the

Introduction

wearing – or rather not wearing – of clothes. That's a completely different kind of streaking and this is not that kind of book.) I have several 'streaks': habits that I've consciously committed to doing daily. Each one reflects an aspect of the person I want to be, physically, mentally, socially and spiritually, and none of them takes too long because otherwise I wouldn't be able to sustain them for the long term.

We know from a vast body of psychological research, such as the work of B. J. Fogg into 'tiny habits'[6] and James Clear's 'atomic habits',[7] that this approach of embedding small changes through regular habits is the best way for most of us to successfully change our lives for the better and to sustain that change.

Once I'd committed to my running streak, something very interesting happened: instead of asking myself, 'Am I going to run today?' to which the answer had all too often in the past been, 'Nah, don't feel like it,' the question I had to ask myself was, 'When am I going to run today?' That's a very different decision. It requires a bit of light planning rather than the heavy machinery of willpower. Because I'm streaking, I'm precommitted, and precommitment is one of the smartest tools in our psychological kitbag when it comes to getting stuff done.

If you think that might work for you, I'd encourage you to experiment with an exploratory writing streak. Make sure you have some way of recording it (Jerry Seinfeld famously puts a cross through each day on his wall calendar; I use the Streaks app; you do you). The point is that seeing an unbroken string of days helps to motivate you not to break the chain.

Why a scruffy pad of paper? I've got lots of really nice notebooks…

I love notebooks. I have several on my shelves that are just too beautiful ever to write in: I'll never have a thought profound enough to justify spoiling their pristine pages. Nobody needs that kind of pressure here. Exploratory writing is raw and messy and honest, and when you start you need to be sure that nobody else is ever going to see it.

For me, the best vehicle for exploratory writing is a big block of recycled lined A4 paper. It's cheap, it's unintimidating, it's temporary, it's unselfconscious and it engages both brain and body in a way that a computer keyboard can only dream about.

So a big yes to beautiful notebooks – but save them for capturing the polished, processed insights that emerge from your exploratory writing, rather than for the exploratory writing itself.

Introduction

And that's it. It's hardly an onerous or expensive list, and it doesn't demand much from you in the way of time commitment or technical expertise. Even if you find that a particular day's exploratory writing attempt was a dead loss, you've lost nothing more than six minutes and a couple of sheets of paper.

You're ready to start. Over the next ten chapters (ten days, if you fancy treating this as a mini-course) you're going to discover ten key principles of exploratory writing and experiment with using them for yourself.

Let's go!

Day 1

Attention

Along with time and energy, attention is perhaps our most precious, scarcest resource when it comes to getting stuff done. And we appear to be in the middle of an attention crisis.

Part of this is pure FOMO (Fear of Missing Out). Choosing to pay attention to one thing means by definition choosing not to pay attention to other things, and when there are so many things out there clamouring for our attention, and so much marketing spend invested in trying to persuade us how essential they are to our happiness, that's not easy.

Another part is our addiction – that's not too strong a word for it – to our devices. I'm sure you've heard the statistics: the average smartphone owner interacts with their phone 2,617 times a day, which doesn't leave time for much else, frankly.[8] Our devices and the apps that run on them are designed by some of the smartest minds on the planet to win ever-increasing amounts of our attention and monetize it, so don't feel bad. The odds are stacked against you – it's not you, it's them. Fixing it, though? Until we get some fit-for-21st-century-purpose tech regulation, that's down to you.

A less talked-about component of the attention crisis is the expectations that others have of us. So often what we intend to achieve on any given day is hijacked by others' demands and, if we're honest, sometimes we're even grateful. Stevie Smith sat at her desk longing for the person from Porlock, the person who (in)famously interrupted Samuel Taylor Coleridge as he feverishly transcribed his drug-fuelled vision to create 'Kubla Khan': 'I am hungry to be interrupted,' she admitted.[9]

And aren't we all, sometimes? It gets us off the hook. If no distraction comes along, we have no excuse not to finish that poem, write that report, find that solution. Maybe that's why we're so addicted to checking our phones: we too long for the person from Porlock, and if they're not going to oblige us by showing up at the door, we'll go looking for them on TikTok.

Write to Think

'Inner work' practices such as meditation can be great ways to help us strengthen focus, but they bring their own challenges. Maybe you can sustain a mental state of calm detachment and oneness with the universe for more than 30 seconds. I know I can't.

But I've discovered that even those who, like me, are suckers for distraction and have an abysmal attention span for purely mental work *can* sustain a focused writing sprint for six minutes. There are two (related) reasons for this:

1. It's offline. Time spent doing exploratory writing with a pen and paper is effectively time off-grid. Nobody can interrupt us remotely; no app can make its bid for our attention; we can't flick to Google to find the answer to a question and then lose an hour to breaking news or, let's face it, cat videos. Just as importantly, nobody can track our keystrokes or access a shared document; we can say whatever we like, free from digital spies. If that feels subversive, it's because it is.
2. It anchors our focus. Inside our heads, thoughts tend to circle endlessly, and as we can only hold one in front of us at any one time it's hard to keep our attention on an idea

Attention

long enough to develop it in any significant way, even at the best of times. And when we *do* have an insight, any distraction – that incoming message alert, for example – can make it evaporate in a second. Thinking onto paper allows us to unspool our thinking and hold on to the thread, rewind if we need to, come back to the point. Whereas thinking often feels like going round in circles, writing gives us the sense of moving forward.

A daily exploratory writing practice allows us to embed focused attention into the day-to-day stuff of life. And that quite simply helps us get more of the stuff that matters done, more quickly.

So what? Over to you…

1. What might it mean if I could manage my attention more effectively?

Attention

2. How could I use exploratory writing to help me sustain attention better?

3. What's most important for me in this section?

Day 2

Instinctive elaboration

What did you have for lunch yesterday?

Just for a few nanoseconds there, you had to stop reading because that question hijacked your brain. You just wasted a tiny part of your life you'll never get back recalling yesterday's lunch. Why? Because of a fascinating mental reflex known as 'instinctive elaboration'.[10]

When it's asked a question, your brain can't help but come up with answers. It can be a good question or a bad, pointless question – instinctive elaboration doesn't distinguish between the two. Most of the time we're barely conscious of the questions we're constantly asking ourselves. Exploratory writing makes them more visible, which helps us get smarter about them. Which is important because dumb questions usually generate dumb answers.

If you ask yourself a question like: 'Why am I so disorganized?' you'll come up with lots of answers, and they're probably all going to be more or less unhelpful.

If you make that question smarter and ask yourself: 'What's one thing I could do today to be more organized?' then you're going to get somewhere. This principle is an essential foundation of exploratory writing because when your thoughts are going round in pointless circles, you can hijack your own brain simply by writing a good question as the prompt for an exploratory writing session.

Instinctive elaboration can therefore be a curse or a superpower; it all depends on the questions we ask ourselves. As Tony Robbins puts it: 'Successful people ask better questions, and as a result, they get better answers.'[11]

I once took our dog Sorcha, an easily distracted springer spaniel/border collie cross, on a gundog training course, where one of the lessons was on retrieval. The instructor stood at a distance with the dummy to be retrieved and dropped it into the grass. My job was to crouch alongside Sorcha and point with my arm to show her the direction she was to

Instinctive elaboration

take to find the dummy. Once I was sure she was lined up right, I released her with a 'go get it!', and watched as she ran straight to the spot. (It took a bit longer to get her to bring it back, of course, but that's out of scope for this metaphor.) The point is that a good prompt question, when chosen consciously and written at the top of a sheet of paper, acts in a similar way, lining your distractable brain up right and unleashing it in the direction of useful answers.

After all, if we're going to have mental reflexes, we might as well use them, right?

So what? Over to you...

1. What kind of questions might be 'good' questions for me?

Instinctive elaboration

2. How can I get better at spotting and ditching the 'dumb' questions I habitually ask myself?

3. What's one really good question I could set myself as a prompt for the situation I'm in right now? (And then of course use it in an exploratory writing sprint!)

Day 3

Inquiry

You discovered yesterday the astonishing power that questions have over your brain. Today we're going to think more deeply about what questions are and how they work in our lives, and specifically about the practice known as 'inquiry'. Inquiry is simply the act of asking questions to which we don't know the answer – or even questions to which we think we *do* know the answer, but which we're open to reconsidering. It's how curiosity expresses itself.

Much of the time, as leaders and experts, or even as teachers, parents, partners and friends, we deal in answers. Other people ask questions of *us*, drawing on our expertise and experience. Our ability to give confident answers about our area of expertise lies at the root of our status and self-image.

Write to Think

Which means questions can be troublesome, particularly in the workplace.

While we remain in our area of competence, where we have more answers than questions, we're in our comfort zone and can work efficiently. When you've put in your 10,000 hours of practice at a skill to achieve mastery, you probably won't be delighted when some newbie comes along and asks why you're doing it like that.

And when we're talking about static skills, that makes sense. The apprentice probably should just shut up and watch the master craft a violin, rather than making suggestions on day one.

But most professional skills in the 21st century aren't static. The pace of disruptive change is so fast that if we spend all our time cosied up with our answers, doing what we've always done, assuming what we've always assumed, one day we'll wake up to find that they and we have become gradually, irrevocably wrong. The solution? Get better at finding and asking questions, aka inquiry.

You used to be great at this. Between the ages of two and five, the average child asks around 40,000 questions – increasingly demanding explanations rather than facts.[12] As Alison Gopnik so eloquently puts it: 'Babies and young children are like the R&D

Inquiry

division of the human species.'[13] There's literally nothing they won't question.

Once they get to school, however, the questions typically tail off. Most teachers prefer to be the ones asking the questions; there's precious little space for curiosity in most classrooms because there's no time to go off-piste. This is changing, at least in more progressive schools. Inquiry-based learning – getting students to ask questions and discover the answers for themselves – is gaining popularity, mainly because it provides a much more effective and engaging way of helping kids understand and retain the lesson. Older students, including those on professional courses, are usually encouraged to engage in reflection, responding to questions focused on how they handled a project and what they might do differently next time. This kind of reflection may also involve research: what's the latest thinking on this? How have others solved the problem? And what additional questions do those answers raise?

But somehow neither our natural childhood curiosity nor what we know about how to develop effective thinking and practice in the formal learning environment typically filter through into most offices. That doesn't mean you can't smuggle inquiry into your own workplace, for yourself and, perhaps more stealthily, for your colleagues.

You may be familiar with inquiry as a tool for self-development in your professional life if you've worked with a coach. A good coach is less about providing answers and much more about asking great questions to help you understand an issue better and create your own solutions.

Sadly, you can't always have a coach in the room with you, but by mastering inquiry as part of an exploratory writing practice you can essentially become your own coach at any moment of the day or, indeed, if it's a particularly chewy situation, night. As Helen Tupper and Sarah Ellis put it, becoming your own coach simply involves developing 'the skill of asking yourself questions to improve self-awareness and prompt positive action'.[14]

The most foundational part of inquiry is of course the question you ask. And not all questions are equal. You probably know already about closed and open questions. When I ask my son, 'Did you have a good day?' when he comes back from school, I typically get a monosyllabic grunt by way of answer. Which is no more than I deserve – it's a lame question. When I remember to ask a more open, more interesting question – 'What's the coolest thing that happened

Inquiry

today?' for example – I get a much more interesting response.

There are questions that are even less helpful: I remember with shame as a teenager shouting at my mother, 'Why do you always spoil everything?' and of course there's no answer to that, just a whole lot of hurt. Most of us have learned not to speak to other people like that by the time we're out of our teens, but for some reason we still use that kind of talk to ourselves: 'What's wrong with me?' 'Why do I always mess up?'

So how can we use exploratory writing to help us ask better questions, of ourselves and of others, so that we get better, more useful answers?

Here's one idea: ask questions of your future self.

If present-day you is stuck on something, present-day you is unlikely to suddenly come up with the answer. Because if it was that easy, you wouldn't be stuck. But future you? Future you has solved this problem – all you need to do is ask how.

So yes, this is a mind trick, but it's an incredibly effective one. It also works in other ways too: you can ask future you about their – your – habits, relationships, day-to-day life, priorities, achievements and more.

There are two keys to this exercise. The first is that you allow yourself to access the *right* future you, the one who has fulfilled your highest potential and purpose. If you're going to benefit from your own hindsight, you might as well pick the version of yourself with the most to teach. The second is that you 'become' that future you for the duration of the exercise, rather than thinking of future you as an 'other'. So as you write, use the present tense to refer to the period you're visiting in the future, whether that's 1, 2, 5 or 20 years from now, and speak about your present-day challenge in the past tense, as something already overcome.

The great thing too is that future you is always available – whenever you feel under-resourced, you can access that fully resourced version of yourself and, by using the power of inquiry, access their (your) strength and wisdom.

While we've been focusing here on inquiry as a tool for exploratory writing, it's so much more than that. As you start to see the benefit of this agenda-free, curious questioning in your exploratory writing practice, I hope you'll also start to use it more in life and work.[15]

Inquiry

✏️ So what? Over to you…

1. How might you use inquiry to coach yourself through an issue you're facing at work right now?

2. How might you use inquiry to help coach someone else in your team through a challenge?

Inquiry

3. What's one really good question I could ask of future me? (And then of course use it in an exploratory writing sprint!)

Day 4

Storytelling

We're all born storytellers. The only way we can process our experience and create sense is through constructing stories, consciously or subconsciously. We tell ourselves stories from the moment we wake up to the moment we go to sleep – and even after that: we're so wired to process the world narratively that we do it in our sleep ('dreaming' is just another word for 'involuntary storytelling').

Right now your brain is engaged in reading this and following my argument (I hope). But if you were to put this book down for a moment and go make yourself a cup of tea – try it, you know you want to – you'd find your brain would quickly switch back to its default mode: chattering away to itself, telling more or less inconsequential stories. The 'autobiographical self' takes over in the absence of anything better to do.[16]

Through stories we rehearse life events and integrate learning. Stories allow us to store more 'stuff' by creating more complex neural pathways (a 1969 study showed that when we hear items presented narratively rather than in a simple list, our long-term recall increases by a factor of up to seven).[17] Stories are maps that allow us to navigate the world, and we simply can't operate without them.

(Incidentally, storytelling is also a key business skill, because creating emotional connection helps us cut through the noise and engage readers' full attention, whereas dry facts simply slide in one ear and out of the other.)

But stories can also be problematic because we start to believe the stories we create, to confuse them with the world as it really is. We want to see patterns, to create certainty. When our emotional brain makes a decision, our rational brain scrambles to make sense of it by creating a story that fits, and we call this 'truth'. 'This is what's happening,' we tell ourselves. 'This is how the world is.'

But of course our only access to the world is through our perception and thoughts. Ask two people to tell you about the same event and you'll hear two very different stories. In such a situation you'd be an observer who could assess the relative 'truth' of those stories, understand why one person responded as they did, perhaps see both sides. But we're not dispassionate observers of our own experience.

Exploratory writing gives us a little time and space to observe our own thoughts and perceptions, to see them for what they are – just a way of understanding the world. As Michael Neill puts it: 'We think we are experiencing reality; we are actually experiencing our thinking.'[18]

Exploratory writing can also help us make our stories visible, which is the first step towards deciding whether or not they're helpful. It also allows us to consider new stories, which give us a glimpse of other possibilities, other choices we could make that might lead to different outcomes. Just as a novelist creates fictional worlds, we can create new possible futures for ourselves on paper, and that act alone can transform our state of mind because it reminds us we have more control than we sometimes think.

Storytelling

✏️ So what? Over to you...

1. Think of a difficult/frustrating situation you're facing. What 'story' are you telling yourself about it?

2. What other stories might be possible? Try telling the story from the perspective of someone else, or future you.

Storytelling

3. What would it mean to become more aware of the fact that the stories you tell yourself aren't necessarily true?

Day 5
Sensemaking

We've just seen that stories are the way that our brains make sense of the world; the wider process by which we construct those stories is known as sensemaking. When we engage in sensemaking we select the elements of experience to which we'll pay attention, and we create relationships between those experiences: B happened because of A; if X, then Y.

So sensemaking is a sort of proto-narrative; it begins simply by noticing and selecting, more or less consciously, what it is we're bringing our attention to.

Sensemaking

Much of our sensemaking happens socially, in conversation with others or within the culture of an organization, and typically without much in the way of conscious thought. Our storytelling brains simply translate 'experience' into 'narrative' without any effort or even awareness on our part.

Because our brains are constantly, busily creating stories out of the raw material of our experience, all too often our instinctive sensemaking becomes unhelpful. We slide into rumination – endless circles of reliving a bad experience, recrimination, blame, regret, anxiety. These old circular ruts that we've ruminated around in for so many years are deeply ingrained, and often the only way to break out of them is to get some speed behind us, which is why exploratory writing is so useful.

In everyday life there are two main ways in which we engage in sensemaking: in our own thinking and in conversation with others. Exploratory writing provides a third, perhaps even more helpful option, as it forces us to articulate our thinking while at the same time allowing us to explore different ideas and their implications without being swayed by others' agendas, judgements or assumptions.

Karl Weick, author of *Sensemaking in Organizations*, noted that writing can play an important role in sensemaking at work: '... there has been an explosion of self-conscious writing about writing styles as tools of persuasion... what most have missed is the use of writing as a tool for comprehension.'[19]

Sensemaking isn't always a simple process. There's rarely a single, clear narrative we can construct quickly to help us understand and accommodate new experience and thereby restore our equilibrium, unless you take the lazy approach: 'Que sera, sera,' perhaps, or 'My horoscope told me to expect arguments today.'

Part of the reason for this is that there are multiple ways of understanding experience, and there are multiple selves within each of us offering competing narratives about what just happened.

Apart from the psychoanalyst's couch, there aren't too many places in the modern world where we're safe to explore these multiple aspects of ourselves. Most of the time we're expected – indeed, we expect ourselves – to offer a coherent view. When someone asks me what I think about something, they expect one opinion that expresses my stance on the matter. The reality of course is that various parts of me might have very different opinions.

Let's put this into a real-world scenario. Imagine you're in a meeting, it's just before lunch, the meeting

Sensemaking

is dragging on and the marketing director has just proposed a change of tactics. The MD asks you: 'Do you agree with that suggestion?' You say, 'Yes.' The decision is made, the meeting ends and you're left feeling dissatisfied and cross with yourself, but you don't quite know why. That night you have a row with your partner and don't sleep well.

That's what it looks like on the outside. On the inside, it went more like this:

'Do I agree with that suggestion?'

Impatient, Hungry You: 'Yes, whatever, just get on with it. I wonder what the quiche of the day is?'

Socially Anxious You: 'I wonder what people are expecting of me here? Should I agree or not? Should I offer an opinion? What will X think if I disagree?'

Politically Motivated You: 'If I say yes to this, Y will be more likely to support the idea I'm pitching next week.'

Thoughtful You: 'It doesn't feel right, but I can't explain why.'

At normal conversation speed, Thoughtful You doesn't get much of a look-in. But taking a few minutes to do an exploratory writing sprint to explore that uneasiness allows Thoughtful You to get to the bottom of that instinctive response. Even just a few minutes spent alone with a sheet of paper over lunch can be enough to allow Thoughtful You to come back into the room and ask to revisit that decision, potentially saving the company from an expensive mistake as well as increasing the chances of you having a more pleasant evening with your partner and a better night's sleep.

In fact, simply recognizing that multiple responses and narratives are possible is important for our wellbeing. It frees us from the tyranny of first thoughts and reminds us that there are always options, even when we can't see them at first glance, and we're rarely as powerless as we think.

So what? Over to you…

1. What narrative have I been telling myself for years that might not be helpful? How else could I make sense of it?

Write to Think

2. Think about a difficult interaction you had recently. What did you tell yourself about the other person? How else might you make sense of it?

3. Think of a version of you that doesn't usually get much airtime (e.g. playful, thoughtful, curious, reflective). How do they feel about something that's on your mind at the moment?

Day 6
Reframing

Reframing simply means changing the way you look at something in order to change your thoughts and feelings about it. It's a fundamental technique in modern CBT (cognitive behaviour therapy) but its roots are older. As Marcus Aurelius put it, 'Reject your sense of injury and the injury itself disappears.'[20]

This is a key element of sensemaking in exploratory writing – deliberately exploring alternative interpretations of our experience. Sounds a bit too vague and mystical? Here's a very simple technique you can use to get started: counterfactuals.

Counterfactuals

The ability to imagine things that are counter to the facts is one of our superpowers as human beings. It's

Reframing

also a curse. When we think counterfactually, we imagine how things could have been if an event had turned out differently, or if we'd taken a different decision.

Typically, we engage in one of two variations of counterfactual thinking: upward or downward.

Upward counterfactuals imagine how things could have been better. They typically involve the phrase 'if only'. Or, as John Greenleaf Whittier more poetically put it, 'For all sad words of tongue and pen, The saddest are these, "It might have been."'[21]

We use upward counterfactual thinking from the mundane, 'If only I'd brought an umbrella,' to the most profound griefs of our lives, 'If only he hadn't got on that plane.'

'If only...' can destroy us. We can never have that moment again; it's too late to do what we might have done. 'If only...' almost always makes us feel worse. But it can make us *do* better. 'If only...'s demonstrate what matters to us, and they may also help us make better choices next time – to speak up, to be bolder, to remember the umbrella.

The other kind of counterfactual thinking is downward: 'at least'. 'At least it's not raining hard,' 'At least I got to tell him I love him.' We imagine how things could have been worse, and we take comfort from that. This kind of thinking makes us feel better, but it can also stop us engaging with the tough learnings.

Both varieties of counterfactuals can be useful in exploratory writing.

Try it for yourself: write as many sentences as you can, as quickly as you can, starting with the words 'If only...'. Don't stop to think, don't censor yourself, don't consider anything as being too trivial or too painful. If you're like most of us, you'll end up with a mixed bag of regrets, ranging from the laughable to the almost unbearable. These are your raw material for the self-coaching questions below.

The first of these questions could be called the 'If Only/At Least Flip'. This is a quick thought experiment that supports mental resilience and can be used on the fly every day as necessary. It works best for low-level regrets, but can be used, with caution, for the bigger-ticket items too. You'll take one of your 'If only' statements and flip it to find a complementary downward counterfactual. For example:

- 'If only I'd checked that email before sending it...'/'At least I didn't copy in the whole company...'
- 'If only I'd listened when they told me he was

Reframing

no good for me...'/'At least I had the sense not to marry him...'
- 'If only I'd prepared the numbers better for the pitch...'/'At least I won't make that mistake next time...'

At one level this is just a simple linguistic trick, but its contribution to resilience and wellbeing can be enormous. Yes, you may find some of these facile, you may even have had a strong impulse to punch anyone who'd tried to offer them as comfort, but they're just as 'true' and just as valid as any 'if only'. And you may discover not just comfort but strength there.

(NB: this works best when you do it for yourself. By all means encourage others to try their own counterfactual flips – although you might not want to use that terminology – but if you push 'at least' down others' throats while they're still in the grip of 'if only', you're unlikely to do much good and may do considerable harm.)

The second question below involves resisting the opportunity to make yourself feel better, and leaning into the regret to see if there's a way it can help you do better in the future.

When I write honestly into an 'If only...', I often find that it is in fact an excuse: 'If only I had the time...', 'If only I could find the right person to help...' These 'If only' statements are not really regrets, they're smokescreens. All too often, if I'm honest, I discover the real issue is something deeper: fear, or simply a failure to prioritize. And that I can do something about.

So what? Over to you...

1. Try out a counterfactual flip. Identify an 'If only...' that's on your mind, and try reframing it as 'At least...' What do you notice?

Reframing

2. Try leaning in to an upward counterfactual and see what it reveals. Take the same 'If only...' statement, or a new one, if you prefer, and do an exploratory sprint to identify what might lie behind it.

Write to Think

3. You can't do much about the past, but you *can* change the future. Think about a decision you're facing and do a writing sprint beginning 'What if...' to explore the possible implications of choosing a particular route. You can do this several times for different possibilities.

Day 7

Empathy

Empathy is defined by the *Collins English Dictionary* as 'the ability to share another person's feelings and emotions as if they were your own'.[22] This isn't just about altruism and being better humans – Google's Project Oxygen and Project Aristotle discovered that empathy was one of the key indicators for its highest-performing employees and teams.[23]

But like anything worthwhile, empathy takes a bit of time and attention. We're so busy focusing on our own needs and experience that it doesn't always come naturally to factor in other people's – but if we do, the results can be extraordinary.

Empathy requires an imaginative leap. By imagining someone else's experience and perspective in an exploratory writing session, we can make connections and see insights and possibilities that can transform our understanding of the other person. It's important to emphasize that the key question here is not whether we're right, necessarily, about the other person's feelings, motivations or experiences – we can never know that. (Let's face it, most of the time we're not really clear about our own feelings and motivations, never mind anyone else's.) The value of writing from the other person's perspective is that we become able to 'see' them more richly and to relate to them more compassionately and thoughtfully; you'd be amazed at what that can achieve in a tricky relationship.

One of the reasons that this is so powerful is that it subverts the 'attribution bias' – our tendency to attribute other people's negative behaviour to disposition – that is, fixed character traits – rather than situation, while we often excuse our own shortcomings as situational. If, for example, we're abrupt with someone, we might excuse it by saying something like, 'I was really busy and stressed that morning.' If someone's abrupt with us, however, we're more likely to think, 'Wow. What a rude person.' Deliberately engaging with someone else's perspective in this way, taking their part, means that we effectively apply this bias in their favour. It

Empathy

reminds us that there are multiple possible narratives in any encounter, which can help us let go of our more unhelpful interpretations. When you get into the habit of seeing those around you with more empathy, and become more willing to attribute their inexplicably irritating behaviours to situational factors rather than labelling them rude, selfish or stupid, it can transform your relationships.

✏️ So what? Over to you...

1. Try it for yourself: find a recent message that made you feel irritated or angry. What might lie behind it? What fears and frustrations might they have? What might they be trying to achieve? Why might this matter to them?

2. After you've written, take a moment to read back and reflect: does what you've considered change your response to the original message, and if so, in what way?

Day 8

Metaphor

'Metaphor' is simply the catch-all term for thinking about one thing in terms of another. There are other terms you might be familiar with that operate in this space too. Similes, such as 'life is like a box of chocolates', are a particular type of metaphor – they explicitly state that there's a similarity, rather than saying 'life *is* a box of chocolates'. But most of our metaphors aren't so self-aware. They're buried so deep in our language and our thinking that most of the time we don't even see them, despite it being almost impossible to construct a sentence without them (there: I just used two digging/building metaphors and a visual one, and I wasn't even trying).

Our reliance on metaphors means that they can be a powerful tool for mental magic if we learn how to make them work for us rather than against us.

Managing metaphors

We use metaphors because they're how our brains work – we find it much easier to think in terms of things we know and experience. We can access what we don't know and express what we can't express in terms of what we do know and what we can express.

That's a massive cognitive benefit. But there's a cognitive cost attached to metaphors too: it's easy to forget that the metaphor isn't actually the thing itself. If we use them intentionally, they can help us be more creative and solve problems, not to mention communicate our ideas more effectively to others. But if we're not aware of them, they can trip us up. Here are three ways metaphors can work against us:

They can generate unhelpful emotions

I'll never forget talking to a woman who was nearly in tears about her situation at work. She told me how she felt she was 'spinning plates', and I could hear in her voice the panicky fear that one day – and soon – one of those plates would fall and smash. No wonder she was stressed. And what a pointless way to spend your day! I invited her to consider whether there were any other metaphors she could use to reflect the way her job involved so many different and competing priorities. We experimented with the idea of her work as a tapestry, drawing in different threads at different times to create the full picture, and it was remarkable to see how this new image transformed her emotional state. This metaphor was calmer, more creative and more purposeful, and she relaxed visibly as she developed it.

They can create conflict

If your idea of being part of an organization is based on a family metaphor, where people look out for each other and the key values are trust, acceptance and belonging, you'll soon find yourself in conflict with someone whose metaphor-in-use is an elite sports team, where you're only as good as your last result. Not until each person has understood the metaphor that underlies the other person's thinking can such conflicts be surfaced and resolved.

They can limit our ability to find solutions

A famous 2011 study by Paul Thibodeau and Lera Boroditsky showed how metaphors can constrain people's thinking about a problem without them realizing it.[24] They ran an experiment in which they talked about urban crime using one of two framing metaphors in each of the research subject groups: to one group they described crime as a disease infecting the city, and to the second they framed it as a beast preying on the city. And then they invited each group to suggest solutions. What they discovered was that even though the subjects weren't aware at a conscious level of the metaphor they'd been given, their solutions reflected that framing. Those in the group where crime had been discussed in terms of a virus took a diagnose/treat/inoculate approach, whereas those exposed to the idea of the preying animal used a capture/enforce/punish logic.

Exploratory writing can help us become more conscious and more curious in exploring the metaphors that we use every day, and to use metaphor more intentionally so that it serves us better.

Once you're aware of the metaphors you're using unconsciously, you can consciously choose to change them. Just as the woman who had seen herself spinning plates decided to think instead

Metaphor

in terms of creating a tapestry from the different threads of her responsibilities, you might decide that instead of seeing your boss swanning around the captain's quarters while you sweat below, it would be more constructive to see them as the cox in the boat you're rowing with your colleagues, keeping an eye on direction and coordinating your efforts. Will it change their behaviour? Not directly, but it will change your attitude, which changes your behaviour, and that's what ultimately changes others' behaviour towards you.

Once you've done this work for yourself, you'll notice that you become more tuned in to metaphors generally (there's another one, look) and better able to spot them in other people's language as well as your own. Which means you're better equipped to understand how those ways of seeing the world are shaping their experience and attitudes. Next time you're talking to someone about something challenging, or you receive a difficult email, get forensic: look for the metaphors in use and think about how they might be influencing their feelings about that situation.

So what? Over to you...

1. Without thinking about it too much, freewrite in response to this prompt: 'My work is...' Then have a go at picking out all the metaphors you've used. Remember they can be hiding in plain view – be ruthless in identifying anything that's not literally true.

2. What do you notice? Is there a dominant metaphor? Which ones strike you as most interesting? Are they helpful or unhelpful? How might they be limiting your thinking or framing your behaviour?

3. Once you're aware of the metaphors you're using unconsciously, you can start to swap them for more helpful ones. Take one of the more unhelpful metaphors you identified above and consider some alternatives. How might they change how you feel and respond?

Day 9
Visual thinking

When we think of writing, we think first and foremost of words.

But why limit ourselves? Drawing, writing, it's all just using the page in the cause of sensemaking. One of the reasons I'm so passionate about using pen(cil) and paper rather than a computer keyboard for exploratory writing is that you can flip effortlessly between lexical and non-lexical marks as your thinking requires. But if you're not used to 'drawing' your thoughts, you might need some convincing as to why it's worth your while, as well as some ideas on how to go about it.

A standard text-based narrative writing sprint takes a basically linear route, however loose – following the thread of a thought, if you like. But

Write to Think

thought isn't always linear, especially if you're not neurotypical, so any technique that allows us to capture thoughts in ways that show the relationships between them in a more spatial way is a valuable addition to your exploratory writing skillset.

Humans are strongly visual creatures: we absorb visual information hundreds or possibly thousands of times faster than written text, and we tend to remember it better too. Adding visual techniques into your exploratory writing practice allows you to access your whole brain, right as well as left hemisphere, and can help you be more creative, identify connections, patterns and relationships between elements, get more clarity about your ideas, and also communicate those ideas more effectively when you're ready to start sharing them.

This is not about creating great art. 'I can't draw' is no excuse. I'm not asking you to channel Picasso in his Blue Period. Having said that, just as writing like nobody's watching helps you be free-er with your ideas, drawing without anyone peering over your shoulder offering an opinion is a liberating experience too. (You might even discover a talent for it, in which case I'd like commission from your first gallery sale, please.) But even if you can't draw the curtains, you *can* put ideas into boxes and draw lines to connect them, and that may be all that's required to give a fresh creative boost to your thinking. Thinking visually means thinking differently about your ideas, and that opens up a whole world of possibilities.

Graphic organizers

Some of these tools will be very familiar to you if you've ever had to present annual results in a PowerPoint presentation – bar charts, pie charts, organizational hierarchies; others will be familiar from books and articles you've read – tables, charts and diagrams.

We generally think of them as ways of organizing data post-hoc, once we're clear on what we're saying, as a tool for communication. But graphic organization is also invaluable for exploratory writing, helping you get clear on the ideas themselves by capturing them in ways that help you understand the relationships between concepts and also generate new connections.

Doing all of these justice would fill a book in itself, so I'm going to focus on two that I've found particularly useful for exploratory writing purposes. And I'm starting with my absolute hands-down favourite: the 2 x 2 matrix, also known as the 'magic quadrant' (no exaggeration, in my opinion).

2 x 2 matrix

The idea here is simply to select two variables, which when you put them together along two axes generate four quadrants or options.

One of the most famous is the Eisenhower matrix, originally developed by General Dwight Eisenhower and popularized by Steven Covey in his book *The 7 Habits of Highly Effective People*.

	Urgent	Not urgent
Important	**DO IT NOW**	**DECIDE**
Not important	**DELEGATE**	**DELETE**

In this example, the two variables used are:

1. Whether something is important or not.
2. Whether it's urgent or not.

And Eisenhower applied a strategy for each quadrant:

- Not urgent/Not important: Delete.
- Urgent/Not important: Delegate.

- Not urgent/Important: Decide – plan to do it.
- Urgent/Important: DO IT NOW!

It's a simple framework to help you assess what's in front of you every day.

Ready to have a go at creating a 2 x 2 matrix of your own? First, a disclaimer: this might work brilliantly, or it might not. If it doesn't, that's okay, we're just exploring here, and even if it's a dismal failure you've only lost six minutes. (But I think it might surprise you.)

Again, pick a live issue for you, your leadership style or professional philosophy, a concept you struggle to explain to clients, anything really, and begin by choosing your two axes – these can either be binary like Eisenhower's (urgent/not urgent) or a continuum (more or less of something).

As with all forms of exploratory writing, it's less useful to sit around thinking about how to start and more useful just to start, so just draw a quick 2 x 2 box and start trying things out – if the first one doesn't work quite right, try another. It's highly unlikely you'll get to a finished article in just six minutes, but it's *very* likely that you'll move your thinking along and get a helpful insight or two, and hopefully also a sketch that you can refine into something more polished in the future.

Don't worry if you find this exercise hard; remember that this isn't about getting the 'right' answer or a high score, it's about expanding your thinking toolkit. But in any case take a moment to reflect on the experience of using a visual model. How was it helpful? How was it challenging? How might you develop your embryonic matrix in the future?

Relationship diagrams

The second type of models we're going to look at in this section are relationship diagrams – remember we're thinking here about lightweight tools to support early-stage exploratory thinking, not the more complex analytical or presentational tools that you might be familiar with if you've ever worked with a business analyst. Keep telling yourself: there's no wrong way to do this. These are intended as springboards rather than templates to copy exactly.

One of the most famous relationship diagrams is the pyramid, as used in Maslow's hierarchy of needs – and I've a favourite slightly irreverent internet take on that.

Visual thinking

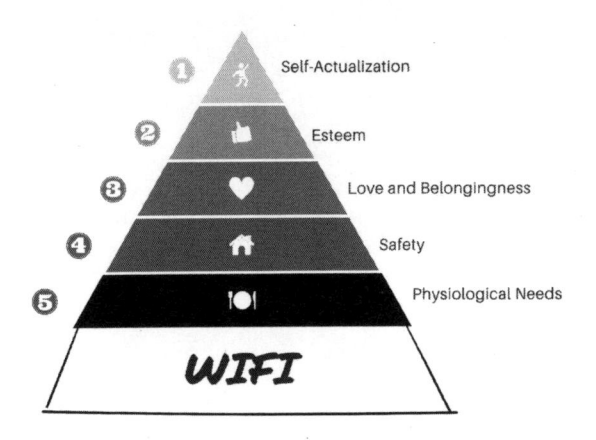

① Self-Actualization
② Esteem
③ Love and Belongingness
④ Safety
⑤ Physiological Needs

WIFI

The pyramid shows a progression from the base to the apex, each higher level accessible only once the one below it is in place. It's useful to express the idea of dependence and increasing complexity or refinement.

Another useful classic is the Venn diagram, which again lends itself beautifully to memes; I've included one I particularly like.

But this is also a useful model for identifying what makes you distinctive when you're thinking about your marketing message. I use a simple Venn diagram to help business authors decide on the topic of their book, using 'my expertise', 'my customers' needs', and 'the future' as the overlapping circles. The point in the middle, where all three circles intersect, is the sweet spot for a business book.

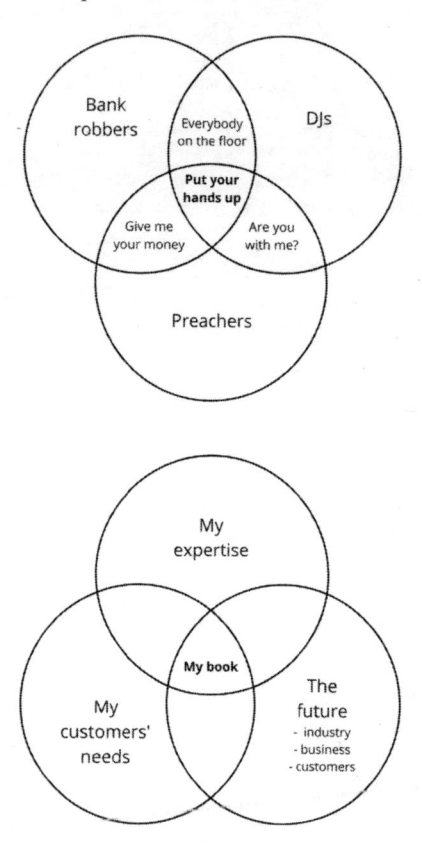

```
        Bank                              DJs
       robbers    Everybody
                  on the floor
                  **Put your
                  hands up**
            Give me        Are you
            your money     with me?

                   Preachers
```

```
                    My
                 expertise

                    **My book**
                                    The
         My                       future
     customers'                  - industry
        needs                   - business
                                - customers
```

Visual thinking

Once you're comfortable using these, you might want to try creating your own unique model. The process of sketching out your ideas visually gives you a different perspective to that of writing them out in a linear way. Not necessarily better, just different, and in the exploratory phase you need as many different ways of understanding your material as possible, because each new angle you try will show you something new and interesting. Using existing models is helpful, but developing your own takes you to a whole new level of clarity, and it means you're not compromising or squashing your ideas to make them fit an existing model.

It's challenging but worthwhile. When it comes to communicating your ideas to other people, being able to show them what you mean visually is massively more impactful and effective than trying to describe it in words. Eric Ries's *The Lean Startup* would never have grown into the movement it has become, for example, without his beautifully simple build/measure/learn cycle diagram.[25]

If you've never used visual thinking in this way before, I hope you'll find it energizing and also insightful. Graphic representation can make us understand ideas more deeply and see connections we hadn't noticed before. And being comfortable experimenting with diagrams like this can supercharge your exploratory practice; the simple act of translating your ideas into a visual representation can't help but enrich and expand your thinking.

And the good news is that your diagrams don't have to be complex. Economist Kate Raworth, author of *Doughnut Economics*, shared with me how her simple but powerful 'doughnut' doodle – a circular band representing the safe and just space for humanity bounded at its outer edge by an 'ecological ceiling' of sustainability and at its inner edge by a 'social foundation' of human wellbeing – transformed the way that people understood her ideas about balancing scarcity and excess by making them visual.

> You could just take the same words that are in the picture. You could write health, education, food, water, climate change, biodiversity loss. You could just write those as two lists and everybody would shrug and say, 'Yeah, I've heard of all of those issues before.' But draw it as a circle, and label them in the circle, and the image itself is doing the work, and people start saying, 'Oh, oh, my goodness. I've always thought of sustainable development like this. I've just never seen the picture before. Now I can have conversations

Visual thinking

and ask questions I felt I couldn't ask.' It really astounded me the power of imagery to open up our thinking.[26]

Developmental biologist John Medina claimed that if we hear a piece of information, three days later we'll remember only 10% of it. If that same information is paired with an explanatory image, that proportion increases dramatically to 65%.[27]

✏️ So what? Over to you...

1. Try sketching a 2 x 2 matrix and/or a Venn diagram as above. What do you notice?

2. Try sketching a relationship diagram as above. What do you notice?

Visual thinking

3. How does this more visual technique differ qualitatively from the exploratory writing techniques you've been exploring so far? What happened to your energy? How did your brain work differently? How could you use that more visual technique alongside the tools you've already discovered?

Day 10
Reflective practice

Reflective practice as an academic and professional tool builds on the work of David Kolb, who famously set out his model of experiential learning as a cycle with four phases:

1. Concrete experience – something happens that demands a non-routine response or challenges your skills.
2. Reflective observation – this is the bit of most interest to us from an exploratory writing perspective. Classic questions you might ask yourself at this stage include: What worked? What failed? Why did that happen? Why did I do what I did, and why did others behave the way they did?

3. Abstract conceptualization – at this point you move on from reflecting on what happened to think about how you might do things differently in the future. How could you improve your response? What resources and ideas might be helpful?
4. Active experimentation – you take your new understanding and ideas about how to do things differently, and you put them into practice. And then the cycle begins all over again as you translate your ideas into concrete experience and reflect on the outcomes.[28]

This is an excellent theory, familiar to every MBA student, but when was the last time someone chatted to you about it at work? Most of us, most of the time, bounce from concrete experience to active experimentation and back. I remember working once alongside a harried project manager who was nearly in tears because she simply couldn't persuade the project sponsor and leadership team to make time for an evaluation meeting at the end of each project phase. This reflection was seen as a luxury they simply didn't have time for, so the project continued to teeter on the edge of disaster and deadlines continued to be missed. (She quit, and who can blame her?)

Write to Think

Donald Schön put his finger firmly on the issue when he described our daily work environment as 'the swampy lowlands' – when we're down there on the ground day by day it's hard to see the big picture; there are no helpful signs to guide us and certainly no paths.[29] We rely, he concluded, on two types of reflection:

1. Reflection-in-action, which is done on the hoof in the swamp, by trial and error.
2. Reflection-on-action, when we retreat to the high ground and reflect on what just happened. This is the core of reflective practice, and it's where learning and development can happen most effectively.

One place in which reflective practice is firmly embedded is academia. If you've studied recently, you'll know that reflecting on your assignments and projects is a core part of your learning experience. Gillie Bolton points out that reflective practice isn't just about improving performance; it's a personal and social responsibility: 'Reflective practice can enable discovery of who and what we are, why we act as we do, and how we can be much more effective... The search for solutions, leading to yet more pertinent

Reflective practice

questions and more learning, leads to unsettling uncertainty: the foundation of all education.'[30]

Finding the time for this kind of reflective practice isn't always easy, but it's always useful. In 2014, researchers from Harvard, Paris and North Carolina attempted to quantify the benefits. They worked with a team of customer service agents in training, encouraging one group to spend 15 minutes at the end of each day reflecting in writing on how the day had gone and the other to spend 15 minutes practising their skills. The reflecting group improved their performance by nearly 25% over their practice-only peers. The researchers concluded that 'the performance outcomes generated by the deliberate attempt to articulate and codify the accumulated prior experience are greater than those generated by the accumulation of additional experience alone'.[31]

Sadly, it's unlikely that anyone is supporting you to embed reflective practice into your own life and work, but that's okay – your new exploratory writing skills mean you can now do it for yourself.

So what? Over to you...

1. Where and how are you practising reflective practice at work right now? How might you develop that?

2. In what ways might developing your reflective practice help you at work, or even at home?

3. How can you support others around you to engage in reflective practice too?

Conclusion

So, is it going too far to call exploratory writing magic? Personally, I don't think so. What else is the right word for a process that makes the invisible visible, that can transform a hopeless situation into an opportunity for growth, and scattered fragments of ideas and impressions into a workable whole?

For me, the most magical part of exploratory writing is the potential it represents. No matter how badly the day has gone, how mired we are in failure or frustration, the blank page represents a new start in a clear space whenever we need it.

I wrote much of this book in Gladstone's Library, a beautiful light space of warm wood and cool stone, lined with thousands of books and where the silence is broken only by an occasional cough or the shuffling of papers. When someone enters the reading room, you can see a physical change: they pause, breathe, slow down. The space, beauty and peace of the room, its quiet atmosphere, create a sense that this is a place for doing work that matters, for focus, for thought.

Write to Think

Sadly, not all of us have access to a room like that whenever we need it. But a blank page? That's always accessible. I've discovered that I can make the scruffiest blank page the mental equivalent of that beautiful quiet space. For a few minutes at least, I can centre, focus, explore the vast library of my mind without interruption, or just breathe, if that's what's required.

So if you've got this far and haven't yet tried it for yourself, now is the moment. Go grab a piece of paper and a pen. I'll wait.

Ready? Take a moment to appreciate the blank page in front of you and what it represents.

Nobody's looking over your shoulder. This is your space. Let it be whatever you need it to be right now, and just write.

Whatever you discovered on the page, acknowledge it. Notice how it feels to have created that space for yourself and come back to it frequently. Before too long you'll find you're carrying that space – that empowering, clarifying, playful, creative space – back into the world with you. And that changes everything.

List of prompts

In addition to the exercises you've already encountered in this book, here are some useful prompts to turn to whenever you need a little inspiration for your exploratory writing session. They're in no particular order, so just pick one at random, set your timer, and get going!

Remember that these are just jumping-off points, and they may be miles away from where you land – that's the whole point! – so don't worry about 'answering' the question; just see where it takes you.

If you have a favourite prompt of your own, why not share it on LinkedIn and tag me?

> What story am I telling myself about this?
>
> What's another way of looking at this?
>
> What would I say to a friend here?
>
> What's most interesting about this?

What question do I need to ask myself right now?

What does success look like today?

If I could have a coaching session with X, what would they say?

If I were a journalist covering my business, what story would I focus on?

What would happen to my business/job if I couldn't type tomorrow?

What have I learned since I wrote this? (e.g. when reviewing the About page on your website or your biography).

What's the quietest part of me saying right now?

What advice do I give others that I really need to take myself?

What's bringing life today?

To me, visibility means...

What can I see, hear, smell, touch, taste right now? (A lovely grounding exercise.)

List of prompts

At my best, I...

Where can I replace perfection with progress this week?

Dear x-year-old me... (write a letter to your younger self, particularly at a time of need or celebration – what do/did you most need to hear?)

Who could help with this?

What do I really want here?

I think the reason I don't know the answer to this is...

What do I need to let go of/say no to today?

What's the truest sentence I can write today?

What small step will make the biggest difference today?

What memory isn't helping me and how can I reimagine it?

If I were writing from the heart and not the ego about this, what would I say?

My superpower is...

The difference I make to this project/meeting/relationship is...

My 'game-changer' today is...

If I had two hours of 'brave time' this week (i.e. when your 'courage' score is temporarily boosted by a factor of 10), what would I do?

What unconscious assumptions/biases are stopping me seeing the full picture here?

When I look back on this week, I want to say...

If I could do that again, I would...

Right now, I'm feeling...

Right now, what's working is...

This week, I'm no longer available for...

Here's what people need to know...

In what way does this thought/action help/hinder me becoming the person I want to be?

Right now, the best part of me is saying...

List of prompts

Whose perspective would be valuable here?

If I could focus on just one thing in my work/life/relationships today, it would be...

Why am I the right person for this task?[32]

How can I move the needle just 1% today?

What's my biggest advantage here? (Follow-up: And am I making full use of it?)

What am I most grateful for today?

What can I celebrate right now?

I used to think... Now I think...[33]

Endnotes

[1] *The Extraordinary Business Book Club* podcast, Episode 245 (http://extraordinarybusinessbooks.com/episode-245-sorting-the-spaghetti-with-dave-coplin/).

[2] *The Extraordinary Business Book Club* podcast, Episode 318 (http://extraordinarybusinessbooks.com/episode-318-the-power-of-regret-with-daniel-h-pink/).

[3] *The Extraordinary Business Book Club* podcast, Episode 308 (http://extraordinarybusinessbooks.com/episode-302-writing-it-all-down-with-cathy-rentzenbrink/).

[4] *The Extraordinary Business Book Club* podcast, Episode 11 (http://extraordinarybusinessbooks.com/ebbc-episode-11-the-space-within-with-michael-neill/).

[5] Gillie Bolton with Russell Delderfield, *Reflective Practice: Writing and professional development*, 5th edition (Sage, 2018).

[6] B. J. Fogg, *Tiny Habits: The small changes that change everything* (Virgin Books, 2020).

[7] James Clear, *Atomic Habits: An easy and proven way to build good habits and break bad ones* (Random House Business, 2018).

[8] Dscout, *Putting a finger on our phone obsession*. https://dscout.com/people-nerds/mobile-touches (accessed 10 August 2022).

Endnotes

[9] Stevie Smith, 'Thoughts about the Person from Porlock' in *Selected Poems* (Penguin Modern Classics, 2002), p. 232.

[10] Center for Decision Sciences, Columbia Business School, *Want to know what your brain does when it hears a question?* Available from https://business.columbia.edu/press-releases/cbs-press-release/want-know-what-your-brain-does-when-it-hears-question (accessed 23 January 2022).

[11] @TonyRobbins on Twitter, 27 June 2017. Available from https://web.archive.org/web/20220810175946/https://twitter.com/TonyRobbins/status/879796310857048064?s=20&t=F05rZAiYz0VzUE3lYgNWwA (accessed 7 July 2022).

[12] Leon Neyfakh, *Are we asking the right questions? Boston Sunday Globe*, IDEAS section, 20 May 2012. Available from www.bostonglobe.com/ideas/2012/05/19/just-ask/k9PATXFdpL6ZmkreSiRYGP/story.html (accessed 3 August 2022).

[13] See her excellent TED talk: 'What do babies think?' Available from www.ted.com/talks/alison_gopnik_what_do_babies_think (accessed 10 August 2022).

[14] Helen Tupper and Sarah Ellis, *You Coach You: How to overcome challenges and take control of your career* (Penguin Business, 2022), p. 11.

[15] Edgar Schein's *Humble Inquiry: The gentle art of asking instead of telling* (Berrett-Koehler Publishers, 2013) is a great starting point. He defines 'humble inquiry' as 'the fine art of drawing someone out, of asking questions to which you do not already know the answer, of building a relationship based on curiosity and interest in the other person' (p. 3).

[16] This term is from psychologist Antonio Damasio's theory of consciousness, and has been widely used elsewhere. See A. R. Damasio, 'Investigating the biology of consciousness', *Philosophical Transactions of the Royal Society*, 353(1377), 1879–1882 (1998).

[17] Gordon H. Bower & Michal C. Clark, 'Narrative stories as mediators for serial learning', *Psychonomic Science*, 14, 181–182 (1969).

[18] Michael Neill, *Living and loving from the inside-out*. Available from www.michaelneill.org/pdfs/Living_and_Loving_From_the_Inside_Out.pdf (accessed 10 August 2022).

[19] Karl Weick, *Sensemaking in Organizations* (Sage, 1995), p. 197.

[20] *Marcus Aurelius, Meditations* – quoted in *Paul Robinson, Military Honour and the Conduct of War: From Ancient Greece to Iraq* (Taylor & Francis, 2006), p. 38.

[21] John Greenleaf Whittier, 'Maud Muller' (1856).

[22] *Collins English Dictionary*, definition of 'empathy'. Available from www.collinsdictionary.com/dictionary/english/empathy (accessed 19 August 2022).

[23] Charles Duhigg, *What Google learned from its quest to build the perfect team*, *The New York Times*, 25 February 2016. Available from www.nytimes.com/2016/02/28/magazine/what-google-learned-from-its-quest-to-build-the-perfect-team.html (accessed 7 July 2022).

[24] Paul H. Thibodeau and Lera Boroditsky, *Metaphors we think with: The role of metaphor in reasoning*, PLoS ONE 2011;6(2), e16782.

https://doi.org/10.1371/journal.pone.0016782 (accessed 16 July 2024).

[25] Eric Ries, *The Lean Startup: How today's entrepreneurs use continuous innovation to create radically successful businesses* (Portfolio Penguin, 2011).

[26] *The Extraordinary Business Book Club* podcast, Episode 98 (http://extraordinarybusinessbooks.com/episode-98-doughnut-economics-with-kate-raworth/)

[27] John Medina, *Brain rule rundown*. Available from http://brainrules.net/vision/ (accessed 10 August 2022). (accessed 16 July 2024).

[28] Kolb, David A., *Experiential Learning: Experience as the source of learning and development* (Prentice Hall, 1984).

[29] Donald Schön, *Educating the Reflective Practitioner: Toward a new design for teaching and learning in the professions* (Jossey-Bass, 1987), p. 42.

[30] Gillie Bolton with Russell Delderfield, *Reflective Practice: Writing and professional development*, 5th edition (Sage, 2018), p. 14.

[31] Giada Di Stefano, Francesca Gino, Gary P. Pisano & Bradley Staats, 'Making experience count: The role of reflection in individual learning', Harvard Business School Working Paper, No. 14-093, March 2014.

[32] This is an example of what Alisa Barcan calls 'afformations': rather than simply repeating a positive statement to yourself, turn it into a question and let your brain find the answers for itself, e.g. 'Why am I the right person to write this book?'

rather than 'I am the right person to write this book'. Yay instinctive elaboration!

[33] Developed as part of the Visible Thinking project at Project Zero, Harvard Graduate School of Education.

Enjoyed this?
Then you'll love...

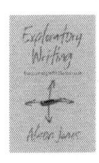

Exploratory Writing: Everyday magic for life and work by Alison Jones

**Business Book Awards 2023 Finalist **
'A really powerful book.' – Bruce Daisley
Simple tools, extraordinary results.

Everything we're learning about how we function best as humans in the digital age is pointing towards one of our oldest technologies: the pen and the page.

Exploratory writing – writing for ourselves, not for others, writing when we don't know exactly what it is we want to say – is one of the most powerful and lightweight thinking tools we have at our disposal. It's also been, until now, one of the most overlooked.

But the world's most influential leaders are increasingly using the techniques in this book to support the key skills of the 21st century – self-mastery, creativity, focus, solution-finding, collaboration – and so can you.

Alison Jones has been helping business leaders identify and articulate what matters over a 30-year career in publishing and as a coach. The founder of Practical Inspiration Publishing and host of *The Extraordinary Business Book Club* podcast and community, she's passionate about the power of writing to change ourselves and the world.

Other 6-Minute Smarts titles

No-Nonsense PR (based on *Hype Yourself* by Lucy Werner)

Do Change Better (based on *How to be a Change Superhero* by Lucinda Carney)

How to be Happy at Work (based on *My Job Isn't Working!* by Michael Brown)

Mastering People Management (based on *Mission: To Manage* by Marianne Page)

Present Like a Pro (based on *Executive Presentations* by Jacqui Harper)

Look out for more titles coming soon! Visit www.practicalinspiration.com for all our latest titles.